# SPACE LIBRARY
# SPACE EXPLORERS
## GREGORY VOGT

# FRANKLIN WATTS
### NEW YORK LONDON TORONTO SYDNEY

Each new generation of humankind has had the challenge of a frontier. The frontier for today's children is outer space; it beckons with unlimited experiences. It is the frontier of my children, and I dedicate this book to them.

Kirsten, Allison and Catherine Vogt

First published in the USA
by Franklin Watts Inc.
387 Park Ave. South
New York, N.Y. 10016

First published in Great Britain in 1990 by
Franklin Watts
96 Leonard Street
London EC2A 4RH

First published in Australia
by Franklin Watts
Australia
14 Mars Road
Lane Cove, NSW 2066

US ISBN: 0-531-10461-3
UK ISBN: 0 86313 637 0
Library of Congress
Catalog Card No: 87-51223

Designed by Michael Cooper

Photographs courtesy of: NASA: pp. 1, 4, 5 (top), 7, 9 (top right and bottom), 10, 11, 12, 13, 14, 15, 16, 17, 18, 19, 20, 21, 22, 23, 27, 28, 29; Tass/Sovfoto: pp. 5 (bottom), 8 (both), 9 (top left), 25 (top); CIT: p. 6; ESA: 24, 25 (bottom); Institute of Space and Astronautical Science: p. 25 (center).

# CONTENTS

# OTHER WORLDS

Exploration is something that humans are very good at. Today, it is almost impossible to find a place on Earth that someone else hasn't been to already. Yet the opportunities for exploration have never been greater now that rocket technology has made it possible for people and machines to fly into space.

Space travel to other worlds is an old dream. Before people even knew that North and South America existed, they were dreaming of traveling to the Moon. In the second century A.D., Lucian of Samosata, a Greek, wrote of a ship that was lifted up from the sea by a whirlwind and eventually carried to the Moon. There the ship's crew met lunar people called "Hippogypi" who rode around on giant three-headed vultures. Lucian's story, which he described as having "not a word of truth throughout," was one of the earliest accounts of space travel.

For centuries people wrote stories of human "conquest" of space with all sorts of fanciful means of transportation to get there. In one story a king on his throne was raised into space by four powerful eagles, each trying to reach the legs of a lamb suspended from sticks just beyond their beaks. Others traveled by geese. A sixteenth-century hero accomplished space travel by riding in a coach drawn by six red horses. In still another adventure, demons carried a traveler to the Moon along the shadow of Earth during an eclipse. A story about Cyrano de Bergerac, the possessor of an oversized nose, had him travel into space by tying many glasses of dew onto himself. Since the sunlight causes dew on grass to rise, large quantities of dew would lift him as well!

**In *Vera Historia*, the Greek Lucian of Samosata wrote of a sailing ship carried to the Moon by a violent whirlwind. Joseph Atterlay's *Voyage to the Moon* described a scientific-instrument-laden spaceship propelled to the Moon by an antigravity material called "lunarium."**

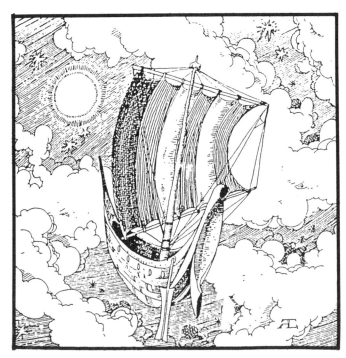

As people began to learn more about real science, the stories of space travel became a bit more believable. A large chute with a powerful spring shot a traveler to the Moon. An electric chariot was invented. Other story writers created antigravity substances they called "Lunarium," "Cavorite" or "Apergy" for lifting up space vehicles. Following the invention of a hot-air balloon in 1783, stories began to appear that used balloons as the means to reach space. Jules Verne, in his story of travel to the Moon, erected a 275 m (900 ft) long cannon that fired a 9,100 kg (20,000 lb) cone-shaped spacecraft.

While storytellers were using birds, balloons, chariots, cannons and dew to raise their intrepid heroes into space, the device that would ultimately make space travel possible was slowly being developed. The rocket began with the invention of black powder. At least as far back as the thirteenth century, the Chinese used black powder packed in small leather cylinders to shoot bamboo arrows. The rush of escaping flames and smoke from the burning powder propelled the arrows and frightened advancing armies. For more than seven hundred years, the study of rocketry progressed—until finally, on April 12, 1961, Soviet cosmonaut Yuri A. Gagarin became the first human being to use a rocket to travel through space. His spaceship was *Vostok 1* and the flight lasted 1 hour and 48 minutes. The fanciful dreams of many generations of writers had finally come true.

**Four red horses pulled a coach to the Moon in *Orlando Furioso*, written by Ludovico Ariosto in the sixteenth century.**

**On April 12, 1961 Yuri Gagarin became the first true space explorer when he rocketed into space for a single orbit around Earth.**

# LOOKING TO THE HEAVENS

Before people started dreaming about traveling through outer space to see the wonders of other worlds, they first had to believe other worlds were actually there. In the beginning, Earth was looked upon as the center of a very small universe. It was the only place with life. All other things were cold, lifeless and dead. The stars above were just tiny lights that possibly represented gods. Mercury, Venus, Mars, Jupiter, Saturn, and even the Moon and Sun were thought to be wandering stars that moved in regular patterns. Because of this regularity, these heavenly bodies were thought to predict and control things that happened on Earth.

For much of recorded history, the exploration of space was conducted with only the human eye and a few measuring tools by people who remained on the surface of Earth. That changed in 1609 when the Italian scientist and mathematician Galileo Galilei developed the astronomical telescope. Galileo did not actually invent the telescope. That was done by a Flemish lens grinder. Galileo, however, realized its potential and built one to look at the heavens. His first telescope was made of two glass lenses held in line by a hollow tube. The first lens bent incoming light from the planets and the second aimed the light into his eye. The arrangement made the object being looked at seem nine times larger. With his telescopes, Galileo saw mountains on the Moon, phases of the planet Venus, spots on the Sun and moons circling Jupiter.

Galileo's telescopes and the ones that followed showed people that outer space offered many worlds to explore. As time went on, larger and larger telescopes were built and telescopes with mirrors were invented. It was discovered that the bigger the diameter of a telescope, the more light it could gather and the farther into space it could see. By the twentieth century, telescopes with mirrors greater than 5 m (200 in) across were constructed. Not only was it possible to see stars and planets, but also great "islands" or galaxies of stars millions of light-years away. (One light-year is approximately 9.66 trillion kilometers or 6 trillion miles in length.)

**Radio telescope operated by the California Institute of Technology.**

The Infrared Astronomical Satellite, developed by The Netherlands, the United Kingdom and NASA, scanned the sky for infrared light sources from its orbit 650 km (400 mi) above Earth.

Helios A, a probe of the Sun developed jointly by NASA and West Germany, undergoes final ground testing before being launched into space in the mid-1970s.

In 1932, a new kind of telescope for exploring space was invented. Karl Jansky of the Bell Telephone Laboratories was trying to find the cause of radio noise interference that was affecting radiotelephone communications. Jansky discovered that the source of the interference was the center of the Milky Way galaxy. From his early research came the science of radio astronomy. Radio waves from space added to the information gathered by astronomers through optical telescopes and helped astronomers prove that the Milky Way galaxy is a great spiral of stars.

Until the past few decades, astronomers faced an important problem in their study of space. Exploring space was like trying to put together a puzzle when most of the parts were missing. Earth's atmosphere acts as a filter that blocks most forms of light coming to Earth. Visible light gets through and so do radio waves, but ultraviolet, X rays, and most infrared light is blocked.

This problem is now being solved by using rockets to launch telescopes and other astronomical instruments above Earth's atmosphere for a clear view. With the new instruments now being used in space, astronomers are beginning to fill in the missing pieces of the puzzle.

# MEASURING THE MOON

The Moon was an important space-travel target for the early science fiction storytellers. The Moon seemed almost reachable; with magic horses, bottled dew, springs or cannons, brave explorers could make the journey and walk on its surface to find demons, dust and "green cheese." When the first real expeditions to the Moon took place, no humans were on board. Instead, rockets fired robot spaceships that were carrying cameras, sample scoops and radio transmitters.

*Luna 1* was the first spacecraft to visit the Moon. It was launched on January 2, 1959 by the Soviet Union. Just 34 hours after it left Earth, *Luna 1* passed to within 6,000 km (3,600 mi) of the Moon's surface and then went on to become the first artificial satellite of the Sun. *Luna 2* followed in September and crash-landed on the Moon. Before its destruction, it radioed back that it did not find a magnetic field or a radiation belt like those Earth has.

Soviet Luna probes continued and *Luna 3* photographed the Moon's far side the next month. In 1963, *Luna 4* went into lunar orbit and in 1966, *Luna 9* became the first spacecraft to make a landing on the Moon and radio back pictures of its surface.

At the same time that the Soviets were probing the Moon, NASA was sending out spacecraft of its own. In 1964, *Ranger 7* shot like a bullet into the lunar surface. On the way there, it transmitted over 4,300 pictures back to Earth. *Rangers 8* and *9* also reached the Moon and sent back an additional 13,000 pictures.

A year later, NASA began its Surveyor spacecraft probes of the lunar surface. In May 1966, *Surveyor 1* successfully landed near the Moon's equator, and four more Surveyors had landed by January 1968. Each had television cameras and some had soil samplers for analyzing the surface chemistry.

While NASA was sending out Surveyors, it was also launching Lunar Orbiters to photograph and map potential landing sites for future Apollo missions. *Lunar Orbiter 1* got as close as 50 km (30 mi) to the Moon's surface and photographed nine potential landing sites.

**(Left) Replica of the Soviet Union's *Luna 9* spacecraft that made the first soft landing on the Moon. (Right) Lunar landscape photograph transmitted to Earth by *Luna 9*.**

The various hard and soft landing probes and orbiting spacecraft helped scientists in the Soviet Union and the United States piece together the first close-up views of the Moon. Telescopes from Earth showed the Moon's near side to be pocked with overlapping craters surrounding relatively large smooth and dark areas called *maria*, or seas. The Rangers and Lunas showed that even the maria had craters, though very shallow and gentle ones. The Surveyors and the Lunas that landed proved that the Moon's surface was hard enough to support landing craft. Years before, many scientists had theorized that the Moon's surface was filled with huge quicksandlike dust pools that would swallow up spacecraft and astronauts. The Surveyors sent back data that indicated the surface to be made up of dark basalt rock like that from volcanoes on Earth. They found thin layers of fine dust coating most surfaces and evidence that erosion was present on the Moon. The American and Soviet orbiters showed that the Moon's far side was very different from the near side. It was totally covered by craters with no maria. The best manned-landing sites were definitely on the near side.

**(Left) Replica of *Luna 10* that achieved orbit around the Moon in 1966 and transmitted data about the Moon for more than a month.**
**(Right) Two years after its 1967 landing on the Moon, the *Surveyor 3* spacecraft was photographed by *Apollo 12* astronauts who landed nearby.**

**This historic photograph of the Moon with Earth in the background was taken by NASA's *Lunar Orbiter 1* on August 23, 1966.**

# "ONE SMALL STEP..."

Robot Moon-explorers proved human explorers could land on the Moon. Between July 1969 and December 1972, six two-astronaut teams walked on the lunar surface, collecting rocks and setting up experiments. They explored the relatively smooth maria and the more rugged highlands. They walked and bounded from place to place and in later flights drove around in Moon buggies.

In September 1970, the Soviets landed *Luna 16* on the Moon. The robot spacecraft took samples and launched a rocket back to Earth with small Moon pieces inside. In November 1970, *Luna 17* landed, carrying a robot car, Lunokhod 1. The car traveled 10.5 km (6.3 mi) and radioed back 20,000 pictures.

The samples, photographs and data collected tell scientists much about the Moon: what it is made of, how its surface formed, its age, and how it probably was created. Surveyor spacecraft indications that basalt rocks underlie the maria were correct. The maria seem to be huge basins—perhaps craters from collisions with asteroids—filled with basalt lava. The highlands and mountains are mostly a grayish rock, anorthosite. Both regions also have rocks called breccia mixed in. These are made of pieces of other rocks fused together by ancient meteorite impacts. Unlike most Earth rocks, which are young and well-worn, Moon rocks are old but fresh-looking. Earth's oldest rocks are about 3.8 billion years old; Moon rocks that age are youngsters. Highland rocks are from 4 to 4.3 billion years old. Earth's water, wind and oxygen wear away rocks. On the Moon, these factors don't exist and 4-billion-year-old rocks look new.

*Apollo 17* **astronaut Harrison Schmitt sits in the lunar rover during the third scientific exploration of the Moon's Taurus-Littrow region.**

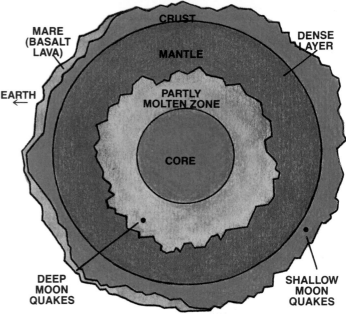

We now know that craters on the Moon are formed by meteorite impacts. Many meteorites are actually small particles that very slowly erode the surface rocks like sandpaper. Only about a centimeter (one-half inch) of surface rock is worn down this way every million or so years.

Some of the experiments the astronauts set up measured the Moon's interior by listening for vibrations when explosions were set off and when spacecraft crashed into its surface. The vibrations have told scientists that the Moon has a very thick crust that extends down as far as 800 km (500 mi). Earth's crust is only about 65 km (40 mi) at its thickest. The Moon may have a small core of iron, and surrounding this core may be a zone of partially molten rock.

Today, scientists are still not entirely sure how the Moon was formed, but the rocks and soil collected by the astronauts give valuable clues. One theory is that the Moon formed from debris left over from the formation of our Solar System four and a half billion years ago. In another theory, the Moon may have been blasted out of Earth during an ancient collision with a giant meteorite. It appears that the Moon itself was blasted with large asteroids more than four billion years ago. The impacts probably scooped out the maria basins and pushed up the highlands and mountains.

**(Left)** Sliced and ground so thinly that light can pass through it, a rock sample from the *Apollo 17* mission reveals its crystalline structure. It is made up of minerals such as feldspar and pyroxene.
**(Right)** Scientific studies of the Moon have pieced together a picture of the Moon's interior showing it to have a thick crust and a core possibly surrounded by a partially molten zone.

**(Left)** An artist's drawing of the approach of a meteorite that may have collided with the Moon during its early history.
**(Right)** Upon impact, the meteorite blasts out a huge crater on the Moon's surface.

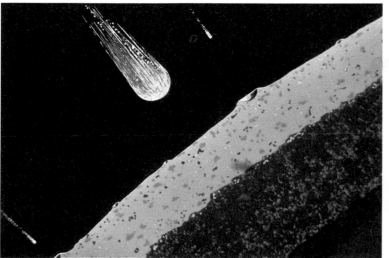

# ROBOT PLANETARY EXPLORERS

Human exploration of outer space is extraordinarily difficult. Not only do human explorers have to carry with them all the oxygen, food, and water they will need, they also have to sever the great gravitational ties that hold them to the surface of Earth. The only way to do that is to sit on the top of a giant rocket and be blasted spaceward.

Getting into Earth orbit is a difficult enough goal to achieve. Travel to the Moon is next to impossible, but even that has now been accomplished. Human travel to the planets is still a very different matter. Placing human explorers on Mars or Jupiter or Saturn is still the stuff of dreams. For now, we have to be content to visit the planets with robot spacecraft that carry electronic eyes and ears.

Sending robot spacecraft to the planets is an ideal way to learn about them. The view through telescopes from the surface of Earth is limited by the atmosphere, which filters out most forms of radiation. Only part of the picture is clear. Spacecraft, however, can travel directly to a planet and land if necessary. They are able to produce pictures at close range with far greater detail than has ever been seen before, measure magnetic fields directly, take their temperature, sample the atmosphere and even "taste" soils and measure surface weather.

As they work, planetary spacecraft radio immense streams of numerical data across millions of kilometers of open space to waiting scientists. Pictures of planetary atmospheres and surfaces are broken down into tiny bits, and converted to brightness numbers that are radioed back for Earth computers to reassemble. Similar things happen with other scientific data.

*Mariner 2*, the first successful mission to another planet, was launched by NASA toward Venus on August 27, 1962. It passed by Venus taking measurements and transmitting data in mid-December.

Since the first successful planetary spacecraft mission to Venus in 1962, spacecraft have visited all of the planets except Pluto. The many planetary missions fall into two categories. The first is the flyby mission. In this kind of flight, the spacecraft, such as the U.S. *Mariner 2* that made the first visit to Venus, merely passes near the planet. *Mariner 2* came within 33,800 km (21,000 mi) of Venus and radioed back data including a surface temperature of 427° C (800° F).

In a second kind of planetary mission, the spacecraft fires a retro-rocket when near the target planet. This slows the spacecraft's speed so that it can be captured by the planet's gravitational pull and swing into orbit. The spacecraft then continues to orbit the planet for long periods and sends back data about the atmosphere and the land surface, if one is visible, much the way Earth weather and land survey satellites do.

Often, orbiting planetary spacecraft carry on-board probes that enter the planet's atmosphere to take measurements and samples on the way down. Some probes are even designed to land on the surface to begin direct investigations.

Getting these different kinds of planetary spacecraft to the proper place often involves interesting orbital trickery. Rockets were not powerful enough to propel the large *Voyager 2* spacecraft to Jupiter, Saturn, Uranus and Neptune. Instead, *Voyager 2* was aimed to approach Jupiter, its first flyby, from behind the planet in its orbit. As it neared the giant planet, Jupiter's gravity grabbed hold of *Voyager* and speeded it up. It actually transferred some of its orbital energy to *Voyager 2* and sent it in the proper direction, toward where Saturn would be three to four years later. This same interplanetary game of leapfrog moved *Voyager 2* from Saturn toward Uranus, and, in 1986, from Uranus toward Neptune.

**The *Voyager 1* planetary spacecraft prior to its 1977 launch.**

**A diagram showing the trajectory of the *Voyager 1* and *2* spacecraft that NASA launched to Jupiter and Saturn. *Voyager 2* has since flown by Uranus and encountered Neptune in 1989.**

# EXPLORING VENUS AND MERCURY

The *Mariner 2* flyby of Venus on December 14, 1962 was just the start in a long series of visits to Earth's nearest neighbor. NASA has sent three Mariner and two Pioneer spacecraft to Venus. One Pioneer went into orbit and another consisted of several probes that separated from a "bus" and entered the atmosphere in five different locations. The last of the Mariners, *Mariner 10,* was a flyby mission that swung by Venus in early 1974 and then went into solar orbit and was able to make the only visits ever to Mercury. Three times in the next twelve months, *Mariner 10* made flybys of Mercury. Pictures it sent back show a heavily cratered surface very much like that of the Moon but hot enough on the Sun side to melt lead.

The Soviet Union has conducted an even more ambitious planetary spacecraft study of Venus. They have sent many Venera spacecraft to the planet. Some have been flyby missions, others have orbited Venus and several have crash- or soft-landed. The early soft-landers had trouble surviving the high temperatures and great pressures of the atmosphere; later landers did survive and transmitted detailed surface pictures. The two Soviet Vega spacecraft that combined visits to Venus and Halley's Comet in 1986 dropped off balloons that floated instruments in the Venusian atmosphere for two days before being destroyed.

Data from the American and Soviet Venus spacecraft tell a story of a very hostile planet. Years before, scientists had believed that Venus was almost Earth's twin. Being closer to the Sun would make it hotter, of course, but it was thought to have a tropical climate like that of Earth's jungles. The spacecraft have shown the planet to be absolutely deadly.

**NASA's *Mariner 10* spacecraft that visited both Venus and Mercury is shown over a model of what the scientists thought the planet Mercury would look like in close-up. Instead, *Mariner 10* discovered a Moon-like surface.**
**The heavily cratered surface of Mercury was photographed by *Mariner 10.***

Foremost in the list of Venusian unpleasantnesses is a very thick and heavy cloudy atmosphere. At its surface, the atmosphere is ninety-one times denser than the atmosphere at the surface of Earth. It is so thick one could almost swim through it. Wind speeds at the surface are a slow 4 kmh (2.4 mph), but they pick up to 350 kmh (210 mph) at the cloud tops. Much of Venus's air is carbon dioxide, the gas animals expel in breathing. In some upper layers there is a high proportion of sulfuric acid present as well.

Seeing the surface of Venus is a problem because of the thick cloud cover that surrounds the planet. The only ways to find out what the surface is like are to send spacecraft with radar into orbit or to its surface with cameras. Both have been done and have revealed much of the surface of Venus to be a rolling plain with elevations changing not much more than 1,000 m (3,300 ft). There are three continent-sized highlands that reach as high as 10.8 km (35,400 ft) above the plain. Sunlight penetrating the thick clouds is trapped so that at the surface the temperature rises to 460° C (860° F). On the night side of the planet, the rocks are so hot they glow. Because of the high surface temperature, no oceans are present. Instead, the surface is made up of volcanic basalt rock turned black by the heat.

Future human space explorers would do well to avoid Venus unless they have some form of submarinelike roving vehicle to ride in that has on-board cooling units. Although a less interesting planet, exploration of the Moon-like Mercury would, in contrast, be relatively easy. Astronauts could actually walk around in Apollo-style space suits, provided they remained on the night side of Mercury or near the line between light and darkness.

**Cloud tops of Venus as seen by NASA's Pioneer Venus Orbiter. It detected high-speed upper atmosphere winds that circle the planet in only four days.**

**Radar-mapping instruments on the Pioneer Venus Orbiter located a giant rift valley on the planet's surface that is 2,250 km (1,400 mi) long. This is an artist's drawing of what the valley on Venus might look like from its rim.**

**Soviet Venera 5 spacecraft that entered Venus's atmosphere on May 16, 1969.**

# THE HOME PLANET

Of all the planets in our Solar System, Earth is the most interesting and certainly the most important to us. Studying other planets is fascinating and gives us clues about the formation of our Solar System. Studying the Earth is a matter of survival; we must understand it if we are to protect it.

Exploration of Earth from space is performed by manned and unmanned spacecraft. The unmanned spacecraft are the satellites that crisscross Earth's surface from 160 km (100 mi) to 35,800 km (23,000 mi) up. Thousands of satellites have been launched since the first satellite went up in 1957.

Generally, there are three kinds of Earth explorer satellites. The first are satellites that look at Earth's atmosphere. The Sun's energy heats the atmosphere, causing it to rise. In colder regions, such as the night side and the polar regions, it falls. This motion transports across Earth large air masses that carry rain and snow and cause daily weather changes. Knowing what the weather is like all over Earth is important for weather forecasting. Weather satellites in high orbits send down pictures that show nearly one-third of Earth's surface at a time. Cloud patterns reveal to weather forecasters what is happening all over Earth.

A second satellite is designed to study Earth's land and water surface. The NASA Landsat and French Spot satellites use sensors to break Earth's surface down into small points of light that are measured for their brightness. The data is transmitted to Earth and assembled by computers into "photographs." Scientists use the photographs to look for mineral and oil deposits, study forests and farmlands, measure the extent of sediments and the spread of plankton in ocean areas, check the growth of cities and monitor pollution.

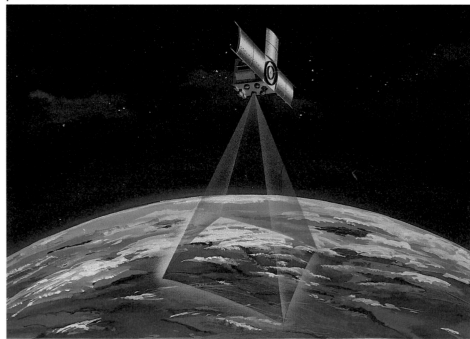

An artist's drawing of the TIROS M satellite scanning Earth's clouds with reflected light during the day. At night infrared sensors are used to detect the heat radiation of cloud patterns.

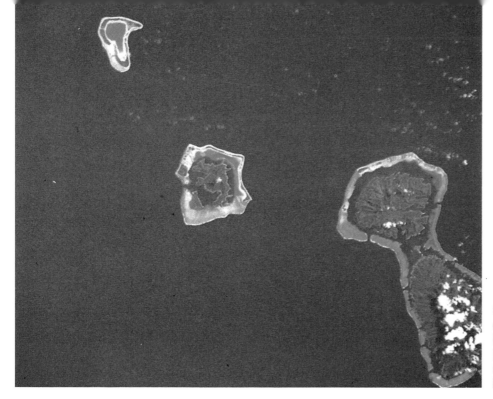

Space Shuttle astronauts in orbit were treated to the beautiful view of the island of Bora Bora (center). The white rings circling each of the islands are coral reefs.

The third kind of satellite offers fewer immediate practical advantages. These are scientific satellites such as the LAGEOS satellite, which is covered with reflector prisms that bounce back laser beams from transmitting stations. The length of time it takes a beam to return is used to measure precise movements in Earth's crust. Eventually, this kind of data may help in predicting earthquakes and volcanic activity. Other scientific satellites measure radiation, magnetic fields and upper atmosphere chemistry.

Whenever a Space Shuttle or a Soyuz space capsule reaches space, the crew inside can look back at Earth to explore its surface and atmosphere. Most manned missions spend part of their orbital time photographing Earth and pointing measuring instruments toward it. The data from Earth-exploring missions has provided a new view of our home planet, including the observation that all nations on Earth are connected. International borders are not visible from space.

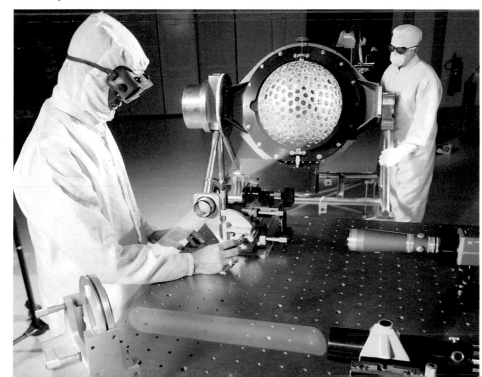

Laboratory technicians use a laser to test the reflector prisms of the LAGEOS satellite. Laser beams bounce off the satellite to enable precise measurements to be taken of Earth movements.

# VISITS TO THE GIANTS

Beyond Mars and the asteroid belt is the realm of the giants. We think Earth is large because we walk on its surface and we can often see its surfaces for great distances. But as far as planets go, Earth is relatively small. Jupiter, for example, has a hurricanelike storm large enough to swallow up two-and-a-half Earths. Saturn has a moon circling it that is one-half Earth's diameter!

Jupiter and Saturn are truly magnificent planets that can only be viewed from a distance. If a spaceship were available to take you to either, you would sink into dense atmospheres that would gradually turn to liquid and perhaps you would never find a surface you would consider solid. Both planets are giant balls of swirling gas.

Jupiter has been visited by robot exploration-spacecraft four times and Saturn three. The first spacecraft to Jupiter was the NASA *Pioneer 10* that swung by the planet on December 3, 1973. *Pioneer 11* followed a year and a day later and then used Jupiter's gravity and orbital momentum to continue on to an encounter with Saturn in 1979. NASA's *Voyager 1* passed Jupiter in March 1979 and then Saturn twenty months later. *Voyager 2* swung by Jupiter in July 1979 and by Saturn twenty-five months later.

The four spacecraft sent back a string of exciting discoveries about the two planets and their moon systems. Jupiter was discovered to have a single ring circling it. The ring was too faint to be seen from Earth by telescopes and was best seen when a Voyager spacecraft passed the planet and then looked back to see sunlight being scattered by the particles in the ring.

Jupiter's surface was shown to be a kaleidoscope of colors moving around the planet in bands and swirling around storm systems. Storms like Jupiter's Great Red Spot were estimated to be centuries old. The bands, called belts (dark) and zones (light), were found to be moving in opposite directions from each other.

**(Left)** From a distance of 43 million km (27 million mi), *Voyager 2*'s imaging system transmitted this picture of Saturn. Details of the planet's atmospheric structure are enhanced with bright colors to make them more visible.

**(Right)** Prior to the Voyagers' encounters with Saturn, scientists believed the planet's ring system consisted of only a few wide rings. The Voyagers detected hundreds or even thousands of very narrow rings circling the planet.

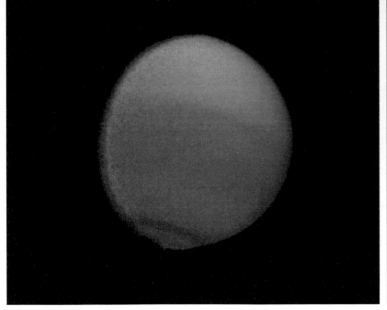

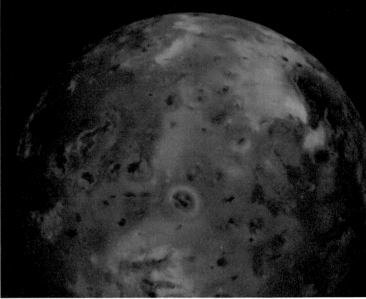

Details of Saturn's atmosphere were not as clear because of blurring effects of the upper gases. The rings were another matter. What was thought to be three or four rings turned out to be a system of hundreds of separate "ringlets." There were even shadows, like the spokes of a bicycle wheel, circling Saturn with the rings.

Great discoveries were also made about the moons orbiting the two gas giants. Many of the moons are heavily cratered like Earth's Moon. Jupiter's Europa is smooth like a billiard ball. Water seeping through cracks seems to have spread out on its surface and then frozen to make the moon smooth. Io looks like a giant orange, yellow and brown pizza.

The moons of Saturn are no less interesting. Titan is large enough for its gravity to hold an atmosphere, made up primarily of nitrogen with a variety of organic gases such as methane. There appears to be enough oxygen, nitrogen, carbon and hydrogen for the chemical processes leading to the creation of life. Titan might be our best hope for finding life elsewhere in our Solar System.

(Left) Saturn's Titan is the only moon in the Solar System with a strong enough gravitational field to hold an atmosphere. *Voyager 2* detected banding and a ring at one pole.

(Right) *Voyager 1*'s images of Jupiter's moon, Io, reminded scientists of pizza. Active volcanoes spew forth sulfurous materials that give it the orangy color.

A *Voyager 1* photo shows Jupiter from 20 million km (12.4 million mi). Io is passing in front of the giant red spot in Jupiter's atmosphere, and Europa is to the right.

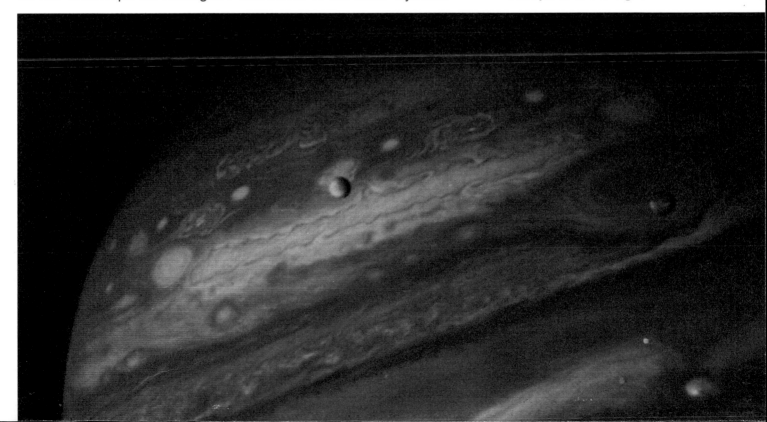

# INTO THE DARKNESS

Following its encounter with Saturn in August 1981, *Voyager 2*'s mission was only half-finished. On its next trip, using the gravity and momentum of Saturn, Voyager was sent on a four-and-a-half-year flight to the planet Uranus.

Uranus had never been visited by any spacecraft before, although an interesting discovery about the planet had been made with a flying telescope two years earlier. The telescope was mounted in a high-flying jet plane to carry it above much of the denser part of Earth's atmosphere. Astronomers were hoping to observe Uranus pass in front of a star. Such events can provide astronomers with interesting details about a planet's atmosphere by the way the star's light is first blurred and then blocked as it passes behind the planet. To their surprise, the star light twinkled off and on five times before it reached Uranus and did the same five more times on the other side of the planet. The astronomers quickly reasoned that what they had seen was the effect of previously unknown rings blocking the star light. Eventually, four more rings were detected.

When *Voyager 2* reached Uranus in January 1986, only one minute ahead of the time set for its arrival almost five years earlier, the rings were one of its important research targets. Would they prove to be like Saturn's rings and be made up of hundreds of ringlets? Immediately a tenth ring was discovered. Voyager sent back data showing that the rings were far less dusty than the rings of Saturn.

*Voyager 2* found that Uranus has a reddish-brown haze at its north pole that is similar to the smog of Los Angeles. Its cloud formations indicate that the planet rotates once every sixteen hours and that it has a magnetic field about one-third as strong as Earth's field. It was also found that instead of five moons circling it, Uranus has at least fifteen.

**Twin pictures of the planet Uranus were taken by *Voyager 2*. The picture on the left was taken in natural color and the picture on the right has been processed by computer to bring out very faint details of the polar region. Concentric rings in the planet's atmosphere are barely visible. The color change at the pole may be due to a smog layer in the atmosphere.**

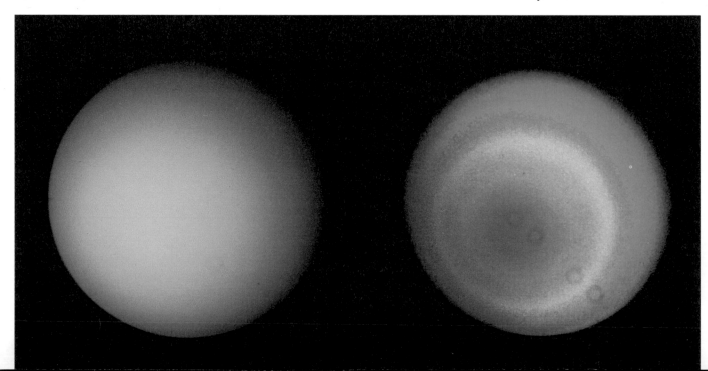

In a stunning completion of its primary mission, *Voyager 2* flew by Neptune; confirming the presence of several rings, at least six new moons, a dark Earth-size storm in the planet's blue atmosphere, and nitrogen-ice volcanoes on the moon, Triton.

As *Voyager 2* whipped by Uranus, it played its old trick again and used the planet to send it on to its last encounter, with Neptune. The trip took three-and-a-half years. *Voyager 2* reached Neptune in 1989, twelve years after leaving Earth.

*Voyager 2*'s job at Neptune was extraordinarily difficult. At a distance of 4.497 billion km (3 billion mi) from the Sun, Neptune receives only 1/2000th the amount of sunlight that Earth does. Neptune pictures sent back by Voyager were very dark and had to be lightened by computer.

After Neptune there is one more planet, Pluto. Through much of its orbit, it is the farthest planet from the Sun. For twenty years of each orbit, it dips inside the orbit of Neptune. It is doing that now and won't be the farthest planet again until 1999. Because of its great distance, no spacecraft has ever visited the ninth planet. When a spacecraft does go there, we may learn whether Pluto should be considered a planet at all. It may be an escaped moon of Neptune.

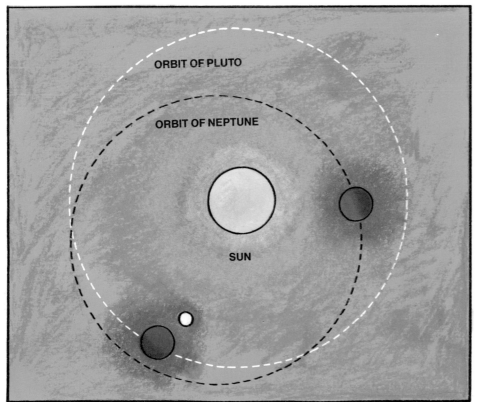

ORBIT OF PLUTO

ORBIT OF NEPTUNE

SUN

The orbits of Neptune and Pluto intersect and on rare occasions Neptune becomes the planet farthest from the Sun.

# WELCOME HOME PARTY

Every seventy-six years the comet returns. Deep in space beyond the orbit of Neptune, the frozen iceball that is Halley's Comet reaches the peak of its cigar-shaped orbit and begins falling back toward the Sun. As it nears and begins to feel the Sun's heat and pressure from the Sun's "wind" of charged particles, evaporating ice and gases form a cloudlike coma around its icy nucleus. A tail of dust and a tail of charged gas particles stream outward for millions of kilometers. Thirty-eight years after starting its inward fall, and glowing in the night sky, it finally whips by the Sun to climb back out in space to its peak and to begin the trip all over again.

Halley's Comet has been orbiting the Sun for at least 2,226 years. Ancient astronomers first noted the comet's passing in 240 B.C. It probably made the trip hundreds of times before but no written records of those visits survive, if any were made.

On February 9, 1986, Halley's Comet swung by the Sun for its thirtieth recorded visit. In previous trips, it journeyed alone. This time a welcoming party was waiting for its return. An armada of robot spacecraft sped out from Earth to greet the comet. Two spacecraft came from the Soviet Union, one from the European Space Agency (ESA), and two from Japan. Other spacecraft, such as the Pioneer Venus in orbit around Venus, turned to watch its passage.

The first spacecraft to meet Halley were the Soviet *Vega 1* and *Vega 2*. They met the comet on March 6 and March 9. *Vega 1* began to feel the comet's presence 35 million km (22 million mi) away when it made contact with gas blown out from its nucleus. At 640,000 km (100,000 mi) it began to feel cometary dust. As it came very close to the nucleus, about 8,890 km (5,500 mi), millions of bits of dust scraped the spacecraft, damaging its solar panels and knocking out two of its instruments. A blurred picture sent back of the nucleus indicated the possibility of two nuclei instead of one. *Vega 2*'s picture a few days later was not much better, but indicated that the nucleus was shaped something like a potato, and that its temperature was about 57° C (135° F).

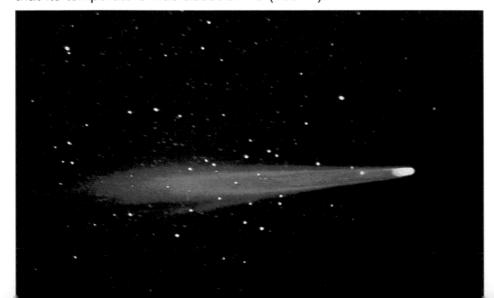

**Computer-enhanced image of Halley's Comet during its 1910 passage of the Sun. The picture was enhanced to bring out detail of the tail structure.**

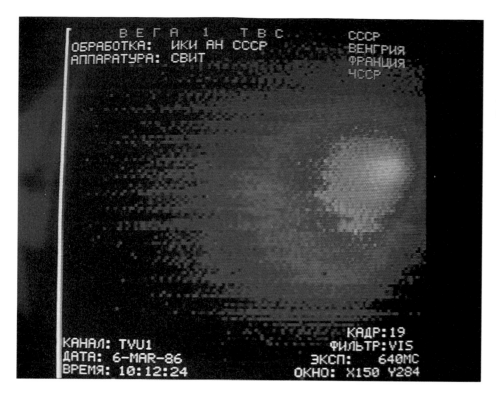

В Е Г А 1 Т В С   СССР
ОБРАБОТКА: ИКИ АН СССР   ВЕНГРИЯ
АППАРАТУРА: СВИТ   ФРАНЦИЯ
ЧССР

КАДР:19
КАНАЛ: TVU1   ФИЛЬТР:VIS
ДАТА: 6-MAR-86   ЭКСП:   640MC
ВРЕМЯ: 10:12:24   ОКНО: X150 Y284

As Halley's Comet approached the Sun in 1986, the *Vega 2* spacecraft shot past the nucleus of the comet, catching a glimpse of a large potato-shaped ice and dust ball.

While the Soviet Vegas were making their close passages, the two Japanese spacecraft remained at great distances. The *Suisei* passed Halley at a distance of 145,000 km (90,000 mi) to study the hydrogen gas cloud around the comet. The *Sakigake* stayed out millions of kilometers away to study the solar wind.

The encounter of ESA's *Giotto* with the comet was very fast. Every second, it got closer to it by 68 km (42 mi). As it shot by on March 14, its cameras radioed back a string of pictures of Halley's nucleus showing cracks on its surface and jets of dust and gas shooting out from it. *Giotto* detected water vapor. Sixty tons of vapor left the comet every second.

Like the Vegas, *Giotto* was damaged by dust particles, and some larger particles even caused the spacecraft to wobble for a time. Its camera system and four scientific instruments were destroyed but the spacecraft had done its job.

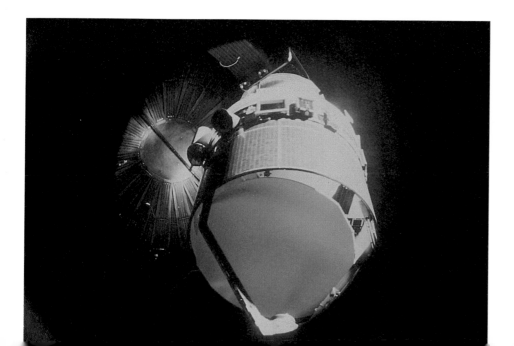

(Above) Japan joined the armada of spacecraft encountering Halley's Comet with the launch of its *Suisei* spacecraft.

(Left) The European Space Agency's *Giotto* spacecraft followed the two Soviet Vega spacecraft for a quick look at Halley's nucleus and to take measurements of the gas and dust traveling with it.

# GIANT EYES

Robot spacecraft have been able to explore our Solar System only as far out as the planet Uranus and, in 1989, Neptune. Pluto and the vastly more distant stars, gas clouds and galaxies are beyond our reach for direct exploration. We are only able to look at these bodies.

If we did have a spaceship with the capability of carrying us out to the stars, it would have to have an entirely new propulsion system capable of moving at the speed of light. At current manned-spacecraft speeds, about 32,000 kmh (20,000 mph), a trip to the nearest star would take somewhere in the range of one billion years.

The best we can do now is to point our various telescopes up and look at the different radiations that deep-space bodies send to us. Even doing that is valuable because much can be learned when telescopes are carried above Earth's atmosphere.

Through the years, many space observatories have been launched into orbit, such as the Infrared Astronomical Satellite and the International Ultraviolet Explorer. Both of these satellites look out into space to see forms of light not detectable by the human eye. Other observatories look for X rays and cosmic rays.

New observatories for exploring space, such as the large and complex Hubble Space Telescope, will be able to peer into space many times farther than is possible with Earth-based telescopes that have to look through the atmosphere. The Space Telescope will be launched by the Space Shuttle. Its 2.4 m (7.7 ft) diameter mirror will be able to provide close-up views of the planet Jupiter that are the equal of those taken by the Voyager spacecraft when they flew by at close range. The Space Telescope will be able to look into deep space and see seven times farther out than was possible before.

NASA's Hubble Space Telescope launched in 1990, will enable astronomers to see seven times deeper into space than is possible with land-based telescopes.

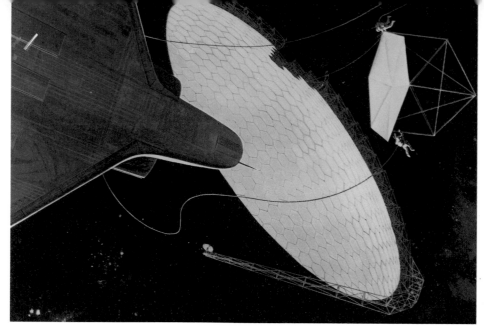

An artist's drawing of the construction process for producing a large radio telescope in orbit above Earth. Two Space Shuttle astronauts maneuver one of the remaining segments into position.

Astronomers are planning the next generation of radio telescopes. Like optical telescopes in which bigger mirrors and lenses gather more light and can see farther, large radio telescopes work better than small ones. In space, large radio antennae do not have to be built out of heavy materials for support. Light weblike structures can be assembled from packages of materials carried on Space Shuttle flights. Space-suited astronauts will extend long masts and supporting spokes like the structure of a giant umbrella. The lightweight mesh filling in the spaces will be stretched tight and the antenna will be ready for service.

Another plan calls for mounting radio telescopes on the Moon. Space experts hope for a permanent colony on the Moon by 2017. Very large radio telescopes could be mounted on the Moon's far side. As that side of the Moon never turns to face Earth, it is ideal for radio astronomy. The Moon will shield the telescope's array of antennae from Earth's jumble of radio signals. Perhaps Moon-based telescopes will detect radio signals produced by intelligent life on a planet circling a distant star.

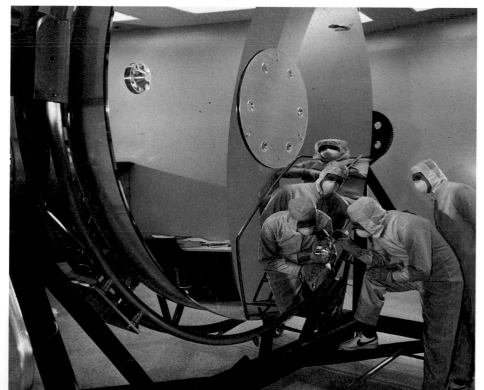

Technicians inspect the highly reflective coating that was applied to the large reflective mirror that forms the heart of NASA's Hubble Space Telescope.

# ON TO MARS

Exploration of space is like the colonizing of North America. First, European explorers sailed across the ocean, stayed in the "New World" briefly, and returned home with stories of their discoveries. Colonists followed and set up permanent settlements. These grew to cities and eventually became separate countries.

In the past thirty years, space has been probed by robot satellites and manned space capsules. The first capsules held a single person. Larger capsules were built and expeditions set out for temporary stays on the Moon. Longer stays became possible when space stations provided temporary orbital homes for a year or more. No permanent colonies have been placed on the Moon, but some space experts are planning them.

By 2017, a permanent lunar colony could be in place. The first step needed is a permanent U.S. space station, now planned for the late 1990s. The station will serve as launching base for shuttle craft carrying building supplies to the Moon. The Moon has raw materials for constructing a colony, but tools and processing equipment will be needed to remove aluminum, titanium, silicon and oxygen from the lunar rock. Small habitation modules, like those used for space stations, will provide quarters for colonists, to be replaced later by larger Moon-built quarters.

At first the lunar colony will depend on Earth for food and water. Greenhouses will be built for growing food. Water will be brought to the Moon as there is none there, nor is there hydrogen to make water with oxygen extracted from rocks. The water will be recycled constantly.

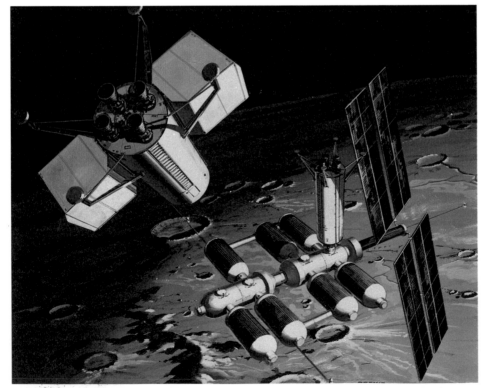

A proposal for a future lunar orbiting space station: The station would consist of interlocking modules serving different functions, such as scientific laboratories and living quarters. A lunar landing craft is docked at the station while another one maneuvers nearby.

In another lunar orbiting station concept, a "ferry" spacecraft prepares to blast out of lunar orbit to return to Earth. The craft shuttles supplies and crew between Earth and the Moon.

While space stations orbit above, a lunar mining operation takes place on the Moon's surface. Valuable construction materials are processed for constructing future lunar bases and orbital stations.

The lunar colony will grow to a city and perhaps an independent world. The people will conduct research and build processing facilities for products too dangerous to make on Earth. Colonists will stay and raise families. Moon children may look different from Earth children. In the low lunar gravity, their bodies may stretch out and perhaps change shape.

The Moon will be the site of the first colony. Mars would come next, perhaps as early as 2027. As no humans have visited Mars, the first step will be to send explorers to its surface. Eventually a Martian shuttle vehicle will be built, like a roller coaster traveling on a loop between Mars and Earth. The shuttle's speed will cut the trip from ten months to just weeks.

The Martian colony will also depend on Earth, but life will be easier. Water can be obtained from polar ice packs and oxygen processed from the thin carbon dioxide atmosphere. The colony will be a collection of clear domes holding a normal Earth environment, with plants and birds and other animals inside.

Colonization of space is one of the long-term goals of space exploration. Russian space scientist Konstantin Tsiolkovsky (1857–1935) put it well when he said, "Earth is the cradle of the Mind. Human beings will not stay in that cradle forever. . . ."

# IMPORTANT DATES

**1609** Galileo uses a telescope to explore the heavens.

**1932** The radio telescope is created.

**October 4, 1957** *Sputnik 1*, the world's first artificial satellite, is launched.

**January 2, 1959** *Luna 1* is launched and passes within 6,000 km (3,720 mi) of the Moon thirty-four hours later.

**September 14, 1959** *Luna 2* crash-lands on the Moon.

**October 4, 1959** *Luna 3* is launched and swings around to take pictures of the Moon's far side.

**April 12, 1961** Yuri Gagarin becomes the first human to explore space.

**December 14, 1962** *Mariner 2* makes the first successful planetary flyby (of Venus).

**April 2, 1963** *Luna 4* is launched and becomes the first spacecraft to orbit the Moon.

**July 28, 1964** *Ranger 7* is launched for a television-picture-taking mission before impacting on the Moon.

**February 3, 1966** *Luna 9* makes the first soft landing on the Moon.

**June 2, 1966** *Surveyor 1* soft-lands on the Moon.

**August 10, 1966** *Lunar Orbiter 1* is launched to the Moon.

**July 20, 1969** *Apollo 11* makes the first manned landing on the Moon.

**September 20, 1969** *Luna 16* lands on the Moon and later rockets home small soil and rock samples.

**September 1, 1970** *Luna 17* lands on the Moon, carrying the robot car Lunokhod 1.

**December 3, 1973** *Pioneer 10* flies by Jupiter.

**July 20, 1976** *Viking 1* lands on Mars.

**March 5, 1979** *Voyager 1* flies by Jupiter.

**December 1, 1979** *Pioneer 11* flies by Saturn.

**January 24, 1986** *Voyager 2* flies by Uranus.

**March 6, 1986** *Vega 1* encounters Halley's Comet.

**March 14, 1986** *Giotto* encounters Halley's Comet.

**August 25, 1989** *Voyager 2* flies by Neptune.

**1994** The year the permanent U.S. space station is expected to become operational.

**2017** The year the first proposed lunar colony is to be established.

**2027** The year the first proposed Martian colony is to be established.

# GLOSSARY

**Anorthosite**–A light gray rock type, consisting primarily of the mineral feldspar, that is found in the highlands region of the Moon.

**Apollo**–The U.S. program that succeeded in landing astronauts on the Moon.

**Asteroids**–Minor planets circling the Sun between the orbits of Mars and Jupiter.

**Basalt**–A dark volcanic rock found primarily in the lowland maria regions of the Moon.

**Breccia**–A rock made up of fragments that were bonded together by the heat and pressure of meteorite impacts on the Moon.

**Coma**–A glowing cloud of gas surrounding the nucleus of a comet.

**Comet**–A chunk of ice and debris that travels around the Sun in a cigar-shaped orbit and forms a glowing coma and tail in the Sun's heat.

**European Space Agency**–A consortium of thirteen nations of Europe joined together to conduct space research and technology applications. The nations are Austria, Belgium, Denmark, France, Germany, Ireland, Italy, The Netherlands, Norway, Spain, Sweden, Switzerland and the United Kingdom.

**Flyby**–A planetary exploration mission in which a spacecraft passes near a planet.

**Giotto**–European Space Agency's spacecraft which observed Halley's Comet.

**LAGEOS**–A U.S. laser-reflecting satellite used for measuring precise distances on Earth.

**Landsat**–A U.S. satellite that takes pictures of Earth's surface.

**Luna**–Soviet spacecraft that investigated the Moon.

**Lunar Orbiter**–A U.S. spacecraft that orbited and photographed the Moon.

**Lunokhod**–A Soviet lunar spacecraft that lands on the Moon and can move about.

**Maria**–Relatively flat and dark areas on the Moon's near side.

**Mariner**–U.S. spacecraft that have been sent to fly-by or orbit Mercury, Venus or Mars.

**Radio Telescope**–A large metal dish used for connecting radio signals from space.

**Pioneer**–A U.S. spacecraft that made the first flyby visits to Jupiter and Saturn.

**Ranger**–U.S. spacecraft that photographed the Moon's surface before crash-landing.

**Sakigake**–One of two Japanese spacecraft sent to study the 1986 passage of Halley's Comet.

**Space Shuttle**–The current U.S. manned spaceship that launches like a rocket, orbits as a spacecraft, and lands back on Earth as an airplane.

**Spot**–A French satellite that takes pictures of Earth's surface.

**Suisei**–One of two Japanese spacecraft sent to study the 1986 passage of Halley's Comet.

**Surveyor**–A U.S. spacecraft that made soft landings on the Moon.

**Telescope**–A device for concentrating and magnifying light from distant objects to make them appear nearer so that they can be studied.

**Vega**–Two Soviet spacecraft that conducted flyby missions of Venus and Halley's Comet.

**Venera**–Soviet spacecraft that investigated the Planet Venus.

**Viking**–U.S. spacecraft that orbited and landed on Mars and conducted investigations searching for life.

**Voyager**–U.S. spacecraft that flew past Jupiter and Saturn. *Voyager 2* also flew past Uranus and Neptune.

# INDEX